THE DREAM OF CHIEF
CRAZY HORSE

David Pownall

THE DREAM OF CHIEF CRAZY HORSE

OBERON BOOKS
LONDON

First published in 1975 by Faber and Faber Ltd.

Reprinted in 2003 by Oberon Books Ltd.
(incorporating Absolute Classics)
521 Caledonian Road, London N7 9RH
Tel: 020 7607 3637 / Fax: 020 7607 3629
e-mail: oberon.books@btinternet.com
www.oberonbooks.com

A catalogue record for this book is available from the British
Library.

ISBN: 1 84002 075 X

Cover illustration: Danusia Schejbal

for Andrew Dale Sanders

No matter how difficult the road,
I will be there: outlasting all wars,
all fire, all hunts, wounds and separations:
enduring as the old earth endures,
strongly, without fear:
I will be there
with you, befriending.
Unending.

from the Oglala Sioux

Characters

GENERAL CROOK

FRIAR DE VALVERDE

CRAZY HORSE

JACQUES CARTIER

THE PEOPLE

SIR WALTER RALEIGH

COLUMBUS

PETER MINUIT

SAILORS

TWO INDIANS

THE TAINOS

EMIGRANTS

ARAWAK INDIAN

FOUR WAMPANOAGS

CORTES

SLAVES

TWO CONQUISTADORS

METACOMET

AMBASSADOR

FRENCH ESTATE AGENT

INTERPRETER

MEXICAN GENERAL

MONTEZUMA

LITTLE CROW

CACIQUE

BLACK KETTLE

CITIZENS OF CEMPOALLA

MANGAS COLORADO

WOVOKA

FIVE AZTEC TRIBUTE-COLLECTORS

CAPTAIN JACK

SATANTA

HEADMEN OF CHOLULA

QUANAH PARKER

PRIEST

JOSEPH

BEARERS

SPOTTED TAIL

THE INCA

BIG FOOT

PIZARRO

STANDING BEAR

CHIEF-IN-HEAD

THE BUFFALO

HUMPED OVER

SITTING BULL

JUDGE DUNDY

AUCTIONEER

This play was commissioned by Rossall Junior School, Fleetwood. The first performance was staged at the Museum Theatre on 28 November 1973 and directed by Tony Brunskill.

ACT ONE

The stage has two levels, upper and lower. Dominating the upper level is a large physical map of the Americas from Cape Horn to Alaska, including the Chukchi Peninsula of Western Siberia. The map must have no political frontiers, towns or man-made designations – only the mountain ranges, rivers, lakes, valleys and plains. As the audience enter the theatre this map is illuminated by the reflected light of a full moon, which is suspended above it.

The lower acting level should be at floor level with the first row of the auditorium. To right and left the lower level develops into two alcoves. The stage right alcove is backed by Stars and Stripes. There is a camp stool and a folding table as used by commanders in the field. A piano stands at the back of the alcove.

The stage left alcove is backed by a par-fleche shield and a war-lance hung with feathers. An assortment of drums and rattles is stacked against the wall. A colourful blanket is spread on the floor.

Only the moon shines. Slowly it dims to total blackout. At the moment when the audience begins to fall silent, a figure pads along the aisle from the rear of the auditorium. He should feel his way forward, step by step. It is CRAZY HORSE, war chief of the Oglala Sioux.

CRAZY HORSE: Shush! Shush! Shush! You are in my dream now. Sleep with me, quiet, shush! Share my dream. Be with me. Help me. Dream.

Silence. Then a loud neighing of a horse. CRAZY HORSE jumps. The horse sounds wild, fearful. The moonlight comes up just enough to show CRAZY HORSE cavorting up the aisle as if he is riding a wild horse.

Hey! Hey! What a horse! See him buck and prance! This is the horse in my dream. I ride him night after night across plain and hill! Hey! Hey! This is my dream-horse. I have not got his government.

CRAZY HORSE mimes dismounting from the wild horse.

And so my friends gave me this name, Crazy Horse. I cannot ride him because he is me. You are part of Crazy Horse's dream for one night and we will see who is the horse. In my dream I can choose my enemy and I can choose my friend. Tonight I choose to dream with you, and I choose to have up here with me my old opponent, General George Crook.

An army bugle sounds. Crashing of feet off-stage right. Enter GENERAL CROOK in full military uniform of United States Army 1886, wearing sabre and revolver. He marches directly to alcove right, halts, about-turns, salutes the Stars and Stripes, about turns, faces the audience.

Soft thudding of a single drum off-stage. CRAZY HORSE pads across to alcove left and sits cross-legged on the blanket. Drum stops.

I have been born, lived, and died. Once I saw the world and now I do not see it. I dream and drag you into my dream. Which is the real world? The Crazy Horse? The Tame Horse? Which story runs straightest?

CRAZY HORSE smiles, then jumps to his feet.

I see you, General Crook Three-Star God Almighty!

GENERAL CROOK: I see you, Chief Crazy Horse.

CRAZY HORSE: You remember me?

GENERAL CROOK: I remember you.

CRAZY HORSE: I have brought you out to play all the Great White Fathers. How does that suit you?

GENERAL CROOK: It suits me well enough.

CRAZY HORSE: Hopo-hook-ahay! Let's go! Tell us how to say the passing of a white man's year.

GENERAL CROOK: January
February
March
April
May
June
July
August
September
October
November
December

CRAZY HORSE: We called it:
The Moon of the Strong Cold
The Moon when the Snow Drifts
The Moon of the Red Grass Appearing
The Moon when the Ponies Shed
The Moon when the Green Grass is Up
The Moon when the Cherries are Ripe
The Moon when the Geese Lose their Feathers
The Moon when the Deer Paw the Earth
The Moon of the Drying Grass
The Moon of the Wild Rice
The Moon of the Rutting Deer
The Moon of the Popping Trees

GENERAL CROOK: You never use one word when a
dozen will do.

CRAZY HORSE: The moon will look well with the stars on
your flag and on your shoulder. One day you will have
the sun as well. It would be right for the white man to
have the sun. It is the colour of his god.

GENERAL CROOK: Dammit man, come on! Let's get
things going! You got me here! If you want me in your
dream then let's not waste my time.

CRAZY HORSE: Your people have thrived, Gray Wolf, they cover the earth and they own it. Mine are scattered, living in the shadows. I see no Sioux where there is power. I only see my people in the pictures that move and they are not as I knew them. Where are my people?

GENERAL CROOK: Take no goddamned notice of writers and scribblers. Stick to the Truth, dammit! Stick to the Truth and you'll be okay.

CRAZY HORSE: It is my dream, Gray Wolf Three Stars Almighty Crook. I asked you into my dream to tell your story. But it is the dream of Crazy Horse and it lives in his head.

GENERAL CROOK: That doesn't worry me. I can look people in the eye.

CRAZY HORSE: There was a word always on your lips, Gray Wolf – honesty.

GENERAL CROOK: Too damn right there was. Honesty is the most important thing there is. If a man is honest then he's all right.

CRAZY HORSE: Honesty we will have, even though it cannot help the dead nations. Honesty is for the white men. They have need of it now. Ghosts do not need honesty. We will be honest for honesty's sake.

Off-stage a soft repetitive chant, 'Hena Waci! Hena Waci!' and the shuffling of many feet. Lights dim. Huddled figures enter from rear of auditorium, heads held low as if battling against a freezing wind. Spot on the map. CRAZY HORSE takes his lance and mounts the upper level. The figures are THE PEOPLE. They shuffle round the stage area, always moving. CRAZY HORSE points to the Bering Strait, the sea between the Chukchi and Seward peninsulas.

Here's where The People crossed. We came out of the cold land to the West, following the beasts. We were hunters and wanderers and we found a bridge of rock that stood in the seas in those days. Why we came I do not know. Perhaps our land had been taken from us in the West, perhaps there were other peoples who made war upon us, perhaps we got lost. But we came across that bridge and we were the first! Thousands upon thousands of turnings of the sun and earth ago, millions of sleeps and wakings, that was when we came into our New World. The Great Spirit was with us, the Sun was our father and the Earth was our mother. We were lucky to find that bridge.

CRAZY HORSE traces the routes with his lance. The chanting quietens.

There was ice on the world in those days and we journeyed through the valleys south, always south. Some stayed in the snow, others went across to the east, some stayed on the plains, some in the forests, some in the wet places, some in the dry. We travelled to the very tip of this great land and we went into it to live. We saw that it belonged to no one but the Great Spirit and the Uncreated Creator who made the Great Spirit. It was only ours because we lived upon it. If we had only known the way of it, we would have got a paper from the Great Spirit...

GENERAL CROOK: (*Butting in.*) However, five hundred years ago, a new philosophy was abroad in Europe, far to the East. It was the beginning of the Age of Discovery, the Age of Humanism, the re-birth of civilisation. Men of restless mind and daring courage looked to the unfound lands...

CRAZY HORSE: Hena waci, hena waci. They come. They come. The People came but that was not coming enough.

THE PEOPLE shuffle off by several exits.

Five hundred years ago the Great Spirit's head hit the blanket, he forgot us and slumbered. The God of The People went to bed.

GENERAL CROOK: The Europeans believed that there was nothing to the west, across the Atlantic Ocean, except, in time, the east.

CRAZY HORSE: Only the whites would come looking for nothing, hoping it would change into something.

Sea sounds, the creaking of timbers, crack of sails, gulls. Bright daylight. COLUMBUS strides to centre-stage, keeping with the roll of the ship, a spy-glass in his hand. He scans the horizon.

GENERAL CROOK: Our bridge was a ship's boards and we came to find out, to see what lay at the end of the world. Curiosity was the wind that blew Columbus towards the islands…

CRAZY HORSE: And gold for kings and queens.

GENERAL CROOK: Dammit, man, he came from a society based on money, which was based on gold. He had been brought up to see things as being useful or useless. He was a practical man.

CRAZY HORSE: He was a thief!

The SAILORS enter stage left and right and mime crowding sail before a good wind. The sounds of the ship's progress increase.

SAILORS: Spain is far behind.
We can only find it
going forward, going forward.
We hope the world is round
and will bring us home again
to Spain.

COLUMBUS: (*Looking through his spy-glass.*) Thank God!

SAILORS: What do you see?

COLUMBUS: India! We have found the other route! Thank God!

COLUMBUS rides the ship's motion like a sailor, his face ecstatic. The SAILORS lower a boat over the side (to the lower level), clamber down rope ladders into it, take up the oars. COLUMBUS boards the boat and stands in the bow. The SAILORS row strongly and sing.

SAILORS: Praise to the Virgin
Star of the sea,
Praise to the Virgin
Motherly, motherly.

Stage right appear the TAINOS, looking towards COLUMBUS and the mimed boat. As the SAILORS sing on, the TAINOS run off-stage and return with fruits and vegetables (potatoes, pineapples, strawberries, beans, pumpkin), pots of chocolate, tobacco leaves (some of the TAINOS are smoking pipes), and put them on the shore. As COLUMBUS lands the TAINOS clap and shout.

TAINOS: Here he comes
over from the East,
the white face
of the sun rising.

The TAINOS shake COLUMBUS's hands, and the hands of the SAILORS. They greet them with great friendliness, pressing their gifts upon them. As the SAILORS and COLUMBUS try out the new fruits and vegetables, the TAINOS crowded round them, CRAZY HORSE speaks to the audience.

CRAZY HORSE: Like most white men of his time, after centuries of wars, rebellions, persecutions, plagues, famines and other unhappinesses, Christopher Columbus did not know where he was going, where he had arrived

17

at, or where he had been when he had gone. But he knew one thing. He was going to be rich, as rich as the Indies. So we were called Los Indios, the Indians – as if there weren't enough Indians in the world already.

GENERAL CROOK: (*Pointing to the map.*) But here is where he had landed, in the Caribbean, the island later named San Salvador. Columbus was impressed with his reception and wrote back to his King:

COLUMBUS moves aside from the crowd and mimes letter-writing (parchment, quill and sand).

COLUMBUS: 'When we landed on this island, the people gave us gifts. I have never encountered a better nation. They are peaceable and good-natured, love their neighbours as themselves, their conversation is sweet and gentle and always illustrated with a smile. Though it is true that they sometimes go about naked, their manners are at all times decorous and respectable.'

COLUMBUS puts the letter inside his shirt, then returns to the SAILORS and the TAINOS.

It is time for us to sleep.

He mimes putting his head on a pillow.

The TAINOS bring out mats and beckon COLUMBUS to lie down. The SAILORS and the TAINOS follow suit. Lights down, moon up. When they are all asleep, COLUMBUS wakens the SAILORS.

(*Whispering.*) Now we must return to Spain. I want to take ten Indians to show the King, with all their gods, gold and jewellery. Raid their village while these are sleeping, then we will take our hosts to the ship.

The SAILORS slip away. COLUMBUS sits apart and waits. Distant cries, gunshots. The TAINOS stir but do not waken.

CRAZY HORSE: The beginning.

GENERAL CROOK: Dammit, man, he had to prove what he had found! Who would believe him without evidence?

CRAZY HORSE: Was he on trial?

COLUMBUS: They must be made to work, sow, be industrious. I will return and see to it that they adopt our ways.

The SAILORS return, loaded with plunder. Then they wake the TAINOS, tie them up, and put them on board the boat. The TAINOS are bewildered but do not fight back. Their astonishment has paralysed them.

SAILORS: Heathens! Anti-Christs! Into the boat! We will take you to the place where steel is made!

The SAILORS row the boat to the ship. As they mime the oar-strokes, COLUMBUS speaks to the audience.

COLUMBUS: And so I returned to Spain, having persuaded ten of my hosts to accompany me. One of them died upon arrival, but not before he was baptized a Christian. I am proud to be able to say that I made it possible for the first Red Indian to enter Heaven.

The SAILORS and the TAINOS go out. GENERAL CROOK gets to his feet. Lights up. Day.

GENERAL CROOK: The Spaniards returned and consolidated their position in the Caribbean. They were courageous, determined men.

CRAZY HORSE: They came back with guns. They came back with priests. They came back with smallpox. They came back to San Salvador and robbed, burned, murdered, pillaged and sold the people into slavery until the Tainos were exterminated – to a man! Then they moved on to the other islands where The People lived and the story was the same again.

Enter COLUMBUS with an ARAWAK INDIAN, a native of the Bahamas. He stands centre-stage.

COLUMBUS: (*To audience.*) Ladies and gentlemen, today we have a splendid specimen of a Bahamas Indian up for public auction. If you examine your catalogue you will see that he is in his prime, free from disease, suffers from no physical disability except his heathen nature, and has already proved his fertility by fathering several children. I personally guarantee that he will work under the whip and, who knows, his buyer may be able to save him for Christ! Think of that! A converted Indian is worth gold in Heaven! Now what am I bid?

From the back of the auditorium come the bids that keep the auction moving. They must be shouted clearly. COLUMBUS conducts the auction with the rapid running speech of the professional auctioneer.

May we have a starter? Now who'll give me a figure? One peso? One peso at the back! Now any advance on one peso for this handsome fellow! Let me hear it! You, sir? You look as though you need some help around the house! We can't let him go for one. Take him down! Two pesos? I have two pesos from the side here. Two pesos? This is ridiculous! Look at him! Look at him! At the peak of fitness! Clean in his habits! Decent! Do I hear three? Three? Yes! At the back there! Three I hear! A wise bid, sir! Three pesos for this paragon of a slave! Are you all finished? You'll let him go for one measly peso, sir? Going for the first time...no? Yes! Four pesos I'm bid. What? Three and a half? No half bids here, sir! We have no half measures! Four pesos? Right! Going for the first time at four! Going for the second time at four! And ...GONE!

The ARAWAK INDIAN is conducted down the aisle by COLUMBUS and handed over to the buyer, who hands over the money. COLUMBUS wanders back, throwing the coins in the air.

CRAZY HORSE: So terrible was the life of The People who lived on these islands once the Spaniards had come, that they were driven to mass suicide to escape from the Hell that the slavers, soldiers and adventurers brought with them. They got one side of the Christian story. The Devil stalked through the Caribbean in Toledo steel armour. Men and women abstained from all sexual life in order that children should not be born into this horror…

GENERAL CROOK: The Spanish military presence was enlarged and a series of fortified ports was constructed. A regular mercantile traffic began with the mother country. Then Mexico was discovered…

CRAZY HORSE: By a slaving-party. Now it was too late. If we had known the future by learning from this Spanish lesson, we would have built a great wall across the Eastern Sea between America and the islands.

GENERAL CROOK: Cortes, a commander of genius, a diplomat of outstanding ability, landed at what later was to be called Vera Cruz in 1519.

CRAZY HORSE: Montezuma, the Aztec emperor, a man raised up above The People until he lived in a world of his own, heard of the landing.

CORTES and two CONQUISTADORS march up the aisle from the rear of the auditorium, their steel feet crashing to a military drum. MONTEZUMA, in a golden robe, enters stage right, covering up his ears. CORTES drills the two CONQUISTADORS.

CORTES: Halt! Draw swords! At the ready! Lunge! Detach! Lunge! Detach! Lunge! Detach! At the heart! Rest easy!

The two CONQUISTADORS stand at ease, hands folded on the pommels of their swords.

We will wait to see what the Emperor of this heathen country will say to my ambassador.

Enter AMBASSADOR and INTERPRETER.

MONTEZUMA: (*Clapping.*) Goodbye.

INTERPRETER: The Emperor, Lord of all, says 'goodbye'.

AMBASSADOR: But I've only just arrived!

INTERPRETER: The Emperor does everything backwards, sir. He is so far above ordinary men that he cannot be expected to behave in the same manner. He sees everything before it happens, such are his godly powers. He knows you will go eventually so he says 'goodbye', to show that your stay must end.

AMBASSADOR: (*With spirit.*) Well, I say 'hello'!

INTERPRETER: The white-face says 'hello'.

MONTEZUMA: Stand up!

INTERPRETER: The Emperor, Lord of all, says 'stand up'!

AMBASSADOR: I am standing up!

INTERPRETER: But you would have to stand up if you were sitting down, which is what you must do.

The AMBASSADOR shakes his head and sits on the floor.

AMBASSADOR: Tell the Emperor that my master, Cortes, a son of Spain and subject of a king across the Eastern Sea, wishes to see all the wonders of Mexico and to visit the capital and be received by Montezuma, the Emperor, himself.

INTERPRETER: Emperor, Lord of all, this man here has not got a master who is not called Cortes who is not a subject of a king who is not across the Eastern Sea, who does not want to see the wonders that are not in Mexico and would hate to visit the capital and be received by Montezuma, the Emperor, yourself.

MONTEZUMA nods vigorously.

The Emperor, Lord of all, says no.

AMBASSADOR: (*Holding his head in his hands.*) To what? What is he saying?

MONTEZUMA: You would be most welcome.

INTERPRETER: You must go away.

MONTEZUMA: I will not give you gifts of treasure.

INTERPRETER: You must take Cortes all the gold and silver you can carry.

MONTEZUMA: And you may stay here for ever.

INTERPRETER: (*Sharply.*) And go back from whence you came.

MONTEZUMA claps. A treasure chest is bought in and opened at the AMBASSADOR's feet. It is full of gold ornaments, silver, jewels. The AMBASSADOR, still shaking his head, takes the chest and leaves. MONTEZUMA looks after him.

MONTEZUMA: Hello.

CORTES and the two CONQUISTADORS mount the upper level. MONTEZUMA exits, nodding.

GENERAL CROOK: And so Montezuma, the Emperor of the great Aztec civilisation, made an error that was to bring down his empire and destroy himself. He gave Cortes a glimpse of the wealth of America.

CRAZY HORSE: He gave him a remedy for a disease of the heart common in men from the East. He gave him gold.

GENERAL CROOK: Cortes ignored Montezuma's order to go away, and kept the treasure and put it in a ship.

CRAZY HORSE: If I could do a trade with the Great Spirit: that I would never have been born if he had never cast gold into the ground, I would do it. I would mine all the gold in the Americas with my teeth and spit it into the sea.

GENERAL CROOK: Then they would dive for it.

CRAZY HORSE: You would dive for it. You cannot disown them, Gray Wolf, they are yours.

GENERAL CROOK: (*Coming down off the upper level.*) I am a soldier, Crazy Horse, like yourself.

CRAZY HORSE: You are a man. Your soldier is only one of your arms and one of your legs. The rest is white man. There's gold in your pocket.

GENERAL CROOK: (*Sitting on his camp stool.*) I obey orders.

CORTES turns to the audience.

CORTES: I was faced by an empire that appeared to be as large as that of my master King Philip. But was I afraid? Of course not. I had guns. I had man-eating dogs. I had armour. I had horses. I had experience. In addition, the Aztec empire was divided within itself, as we found when we entered the city of Cempoalla.

Enter CACIQUE of Cempoalla.

CACIQUE: (*In a state of terror.*) Two legs! Two legs! He has two legs! Two legs! Only two legs!

Enter CITIZENS, who gather round CACIQUE pointing, shouting.

CITIZENS: Two legs! Only two legs! Ah, only two!

CORTES: (*Slapping each thigh.*) One! Two! That's all! Why is that such a marvel!

CACIQUE: We were told that you were four-legged giants with human halves. We saw you from a distance on the road and that is what you were. Now you are a man.

CORTES: (*Aside to the audience.*) You see how easy it was?

CACIQUE: You have a powerful god. One minute you are one thing, the next, another.

CORTES: We ride horses. The horse is an animal. It is a beast of the field that will yield to a man on its back.

CITIZENS: Ah! A horse! A horse!

CORTES: We are riding to see Montezuma.

Pause. The CACIQUE tightens his lip. The CITIZENS go sullen.

CACIQUE: You will give him horses? Give us horses instead. We are your friends.

Enter five Aztec TRIBUTE-COLLECTORS richly clad, haughty, holding bunches of flowers and followed by attendants with fans. The Aztec TRIBUTE-COLLECTORS talk in sequence, phrase by phrase. CORTES exits.

FIRST TRIBUTE-COLLECTOR: You must not help

SECOND TRIBUTE-COLLECTOR: the Easterners without

THIRD TRIBUTE-COLLECTOR: express permission

FOURTH TRIBUTE-COLLECTOR: from the Emperor

FIFTH TRIBUTE-COLLECTOR: Who wants them to

FIRST TRIBUTE-COLLECTOR: go away.

CACIQUE: (*Fearfully.*) We have given them no help! We are loyal to the Emperor Montezuma! The people of Cempoalla, the nation of the Totonac, obey the Emperor's word!

FIRST TRIBUTE-COLLECTOR: The Emperor has heard

SECOND TRIBUTE-COLLECTOR: that you are prepared

THIRD TRIBUTE-COLLECTOR: to revolt against him.

FOURTH TRIBUTE-COLLECTOR: We demand a tribute of twenty

FIFTH TRIBUTE-COLLECTOR: young men and women for sacrifice.

CACIQUE: We are a poor city. You take the best of our youth for the altars of Tenochtitlan. The gods are not that hungry.

Re-enter CORTES.

CORTES: (*To CACIQUE.*) Put them in prison.

CACIQUE: The Emperor's tribute-collectors?

CORTES: What right has he to demand the lives of your people? What a barbarian he must be! Human sacrifice is the worst crime in the world. Hasn't anybody told you?

CACIQUE: (*To the CITIZENS.*) What do you say?

CITIZENS: Lock them up! Away! Away!

The TRIBUTE-COLLECTORS and their attendants are grabbed.

FIRST TRIBUTE-COLLECTOR: Oooh! You'll

SECOND TRIBUTE-COLLECTOR: Aaah! never

THIRD TRIBUTE-COLLECTOR: Groo! get

FOURTH TRIBUTE-COLLECTOR: Aieee! away

FIFTH TRIBUTE-COLLECTOR: Help! with this!

The TRIBUTE-COLLECTORS are bundled off. Lights down. Moon up. CORTES exits, then re-appears, wiping his sword, followed by three TRIBUTE-COLLECTORS.

CORTES: There we are. I arranged your release.

FIRST TRIBUTE-COLLECTOR: We are grateful.

SECOND TRIBUTE-COLLECTOR: but for your timely

THIRD TRIBUTE-COLLECTOR: intervention

FIRST TRIBUTE-COLLECTOR: these treacherous Totonacs

SECOND TRIBUTE-COLLECTOR: would have surely killed us.

Enter CACIQUE. Noises off, CITIZENS in an uproar.

CACIQUE: So you're still here!

CORTES: I caught them trying to escape.

CACIQUE: They murdered the guards! Now we will sacrifice them!

CORTES: They are my prisoners now. I abhor human sacrifice.

CACIQUE: Then may we sacrifice the two that we have got left still in prison? That would be a reasonable compromise.

FIRST TRIBUTE-COLLECTOR: We must protest

SECOND TRIBUTE-COLLECTOR: in the strongest possible terms

THIRD TRIBUTE-COLLECTOR: about the way we are

FIRST TRIBUTE-COLLECTOR: being used as pawns

SECOND TRIBUTE-COLLECTOR: in a political game.

CORTES: If you will release the Tribute-Collectors into my care I will return them to the Emperor and ask for your nation to be allowed to govern itself as a sovereign state. Montezuma will listen to me. With my arms, my armour and my horses, I will be your spokesman and your ally. I will buy your road to Freedom.

Exit CORTES with the FIRST, SECOND and THIRD TRIBUTE-COLLECTORS. The CACIQUE remains behind, scratching his head.

CACIQUE: Perhaps it is me that is the beast of burden? Am I a horse? Who is riding me to Montezuma?

CACIQUE exits. GENERAL CROOK sits down on his camp-stool.

GENERAL CROOK: Cortes then climbed to the high plateau of Mexico and fought the Tascalan nation, with steel and words, until they became horses too and agreed to help Cortes overthrow the Aztec. Human sacrifice had to be stamped out.

CRAZY HORSE: (*Laughing.*) How many men are you, Gray Wolf? You speak twice for every one word. Human sacrifice!

GENERAL CROOK: You Indians practised every damned perversion in the book. Cannibalism! The Iroquois ate their enemies for strength!

CRAZY HORSE: Who ate Jesus for strength? Ha!

GENERAL CROOK: That was our religion.

CRAZY HORSE: Does that make it better?

GENERAL CROOK: The Apache were the cruellest torturers I've ever encountered. God, the things they did to their victims turned my guts up!

CRAZY HORSE: They learned well from the Spaniards. The Spaniards taught them to fight fire with fire.

GENERAL CROOK: Slavery, you say. You Indians had slaves!

CRAZY HORSE: Prisoners of war.

GENERAL CROOK: Pah! Women and children? Prisoners of war?

CRAZY HORSE: We never paid gold for men. No Indian ever bought a man.

GENERAL CROOK: You never had any gold. You hadn't got the goddamned sense to dig up what was on your own doorstep!

CRAZY HORSE: Gold was part of the earth, Gray Wolf. It was not the whole meaning of the earth as it was with your people.

CRAZY HORSE tightens his lip and stares at the floor, then looks up.

Then the people of Cholula, a city of twenty thousand buildings, asked Cortes to visit them. Like the Totonacs they were tired of Montezuma's tyranny and wanted a treaty with the powerful Spaniard. Cortes came.

The HEADMEN OF CHOLULA enter from all sides except the aisle. They are unarmed. As they enter they sing.

HEADMEN OF CHOLULA:
We have heard of the black powder! Ha!
We have heard of the hair on the face! Ha!
Like the black thunder-cloud from the East.
We have heard the white man coming.

CORTES enters with his two CONQUISTADORS from the rear of the auditorium, and marches up to the HEADMEN OF CHOLULA. The two CONQUISTADORS cover the stage right and left exits. The HEADMEN admire their guns, swords and armour and try to touch them. The TWO CONQUISTADORS fend them off.

CORTES mounts the upper level, then herds all the HEADMEN OF CHOLULA on to the lower level.

CORTES: Give me room! Give me space! The air stinks! Stand back! I have a man to talk to you! Listen to him well!

HEADMEN OF CHOLULA:
We came to see the horse!
We came to see the strong metal!
We came to be free!

Enter PRIEST, a Jesuit in black.

CORTES: Here is the man to make you free!

HEADMEN OF CHOLULA:
We have heard of the black white
And the grey words of his mouth!
We are here for arms, not tongues!

The HEADMEN OF CHOLULA start to leave but they are stopped by the TWO CONQUISTADORS. They retreat, grumbling.

PRIEST: I have come here to point out the Truth. It is not in your Emperor. It is not in your gods. The Truth lies in the god we have found. His way is the way of love and vengeance, Heaven and Hell. He is three in one and one in three.

FIRST HEADMAN: This man talks like the Emperor!

SECOND HEADMAN: Goodbye!

THIRD HEADMAN: Hello!

PRIEST: (*Angrily.*) The punishment of sin is Hell and the heathen lives in a state of perpetual sin. His foot contaminates the earth he walks upon, his breath pollutes the air he breathes. His life is a poisoned river! You must turn to Christ to be saved. Your souls are in peril. You are tinder too near the flame!

HEADMEN OF CHOLULA: Take the crow away! Fly to another tree! No more talk! We have gods! Our gods understand us!

CORTES: Quiet! This is a man of God, an ordained priest! You must respect him!

PRIEST: If you would have God's mercy, then be baptized by me. All those who would enter the Kingdom of Heaven, come up to me and I will open the gate! Hear the call! Do not rot in your heathen ways! God beckons you!

The PRIEST opens his arms. The HEADMEN OF CHOLULA do not respond. Silence. CORTES fumes. He looks menacingly at the two CONQUISTADORS, who level their arquebuses at the HEADMEN.

You are unclean and I offer you water. I am the spiritual power of the East and I carry mercy in my bag. Give me a chance to save you. If you reject my word, then the power of the temporal world must have you. I must hand you over to the brush to be swept away. This is your last chance to live. Take it! (*Silence. The PRIEST glares wildly at the HEADMEN.*) Then perish and be damned!

Blackout. Explosions all round the stage and auditorium. Screams, mayhem. Five seconds of noisy, earsplitting chaos. Then silence again. Lights up. The HEADMEN OF CHOLULA lie heaped on the lower level, one on top of the other. CORTES and the TWO CONQUISTADORS lean on their swords, exhausted with slaughter.

31

CORTES: We have done great work for God. There will be no more human sacrifice here.

PRIEST: God's will is done.

As GENERAL CROOK and CRAZY HORSE take up the story, the HEADMEN OF CHOLULA get up and slip away, followed by CORTES, the PRIEST and the two CONQUISTADORS. Lights dim as they go, the moon shines again.

GENERAL CROOK: So Cortes went on from victory to victory, sweeping all before him. His allies multiplied daily as his reputation spread.

CRAZY HORSE: He galloped on towards Montezuma's capital astride the new American horse, civil war. There the Emperor, the man who had given Cortes pennies to go away like a bad musician, was forced to yield up his power and his gold.

GENERAL CROOK: Montezuma stood on one of the great Aztec pyramids and looked down on his capital...

Enter MONTEZUMA; he stands centre upper-level. CORTES enters at the rear of the auditorium and mimes the climbing of a giant pyramid, step by step, the two CONQUISTADORS behind him.

FIRST CONQUISTADOR: (*Looking up at MONTEZUMA.*) Who does he think he is?

SECOND CONQUISTADOR: Old Cortes will soon bring him down to earth.

FIRST CONQUISTADOR: By the Virgin, they could build. But they can't fight, eh? So he's the one close to the gods.

SECOND CONQUISTADOR: He'll soon be closer than he thinks.

MONTEZUMA: I am happy to see you. Welcome. Thank you kindly for laying waste my empire, stirring up insurrection and civil war, massacring my people and looting my treasuries. I really am most grateful. I hope you are not finding the ascent painful?

CORTES: (*Panting.*) Surrender!

MONTEZUMA: Pause, look about you, there is Mexico. It is not yours.

CORTES: You are my prisoner.

MONTEZUMA: I am free.

CORTES reaches the top of the pyramid. MONTEZUMA holds out his wrists for a chain.

And you do not exist. You are where you came from, across the Eastern Sea. You will not put my city to the sword, you will not murder me. Everything is wonderful. I declare before my gods, there is not a happier man alive than Montezuma.

Pause. MONTEZUMA sees Mexico as it is for the first time, the scales fall from his eyes.

Goodbye.

The two CONQUISTADORS lead MONTEZUMA off right. CORTES stands, hands on hips, surveying the world he has won.

CORTES: I have done it. I, I, I. This is mine!

The PRIEST pokes his head around the map.

PRIEST: And mine, brother-in-Christ.

CORTES exits. Lights dim. Spots on GENERAL CROOK and CRAZY HORSE.

GENERAL CROOK: The campaign was over. Mexico became New Spain and a part of the Spanish Empire. As a war of conquest it was a tremendous example to future strategists and thinkers specialising in the military arts. Divide and rule. Go for the top. Advance, advance. Be audacious. Arms make the man. Surprise. Terrify. Destroy to build again.

CRAZY HORSE: The disease worse than smallpox was with us.

GENERAL CROOK: The new leader of America. Not emperors, not kings, not aristocrats, but the supreme individualist, the figurehead of Free Enterprise.

CRAZY HORSE: It was not over. Far to the south where The People had drifted there was another empire.

GENERAL CROOK: (*Mounting the upper level. Spot on map.*) Here (*He points with his sabre.*) in what is now Peru, the Inca ruled five million of his subjects much as Montezuma had once ruled his.

CRAZY HORSE: With one difference. This Inca was not only a great man, but he was also god. He had learnt the ways of the white man before he had seen them. He was the Sun, he warmed the earth.

GENERAL CROOK: The administration of the Inca empire was unparalleled. They were the Romans of the Americas.

CRAZY HORSE: The Inca empire had survived three hundred years, built great cities, roads, a government never to be seen again in South America. As slaves of the Sun, the Incas were the freest men on Earth.

GENERAL CROOK sheathes his sabre and returns to his alcove. Great burst of light. Crash of cymbals, roar of drums, trumpets blow. A golden litter with drawn curtains enters from the rear of the auditorium, carried by BEARERS. As the BEARERS carry the litter down the aisle they shout.

BEARERS: Most High Lord!
Child and Father of the Sun!
Our Sole and Beloved Lord!
Shine on! Shine on!

CRAZY HORSE: Ten years after the conquest of Mexico, the Sun himself, the holy Inca, was in danger. Through the Andes came one-hundred-and-seventeen Spanish soldiers led by an unlettered criminal, Pizarro. They were looking for gold, the colour of the Sun.

Enter PIZARRO and two CONQUISTADORS stage left, as if climbing a mountain. The INCA's litter is carried forward slowly, the BEARERS chanting. PIZARRO and the two CONQUISTADORS reach the top of the mountain and sit down, looking across to the litter.

PIZARRO: He is coming!

CRAZY HORSE: From the time that they began their advance into the Inca's Kingdom Pizarro and his men had received nothing but hospitality. They could have been wiped out at any time but the Inca treated them like honoured guests. It was the story of the Tainos all over again.

GENERAL CROOK: The Inca was staying at Caxamalca and agreed to leave the city to visit Pizarro in his camp. With the heads of his government and thousands of his followers…

CRAZY HORSE: All unarmed…

GENERAL CROOK: …The Inca entered the Spanish expedition's quarters.

PIZARRO and the two CONQUISTADORS mime running down the mountain and go out. The INCA arrives at the upper level of the stage and the litter is put down. The INCA remains in the litter with the curtains drawn. PIZARRO and the two CONQUISTADORS are seen hiding, armed, stage left and right. FRIAR DE VALVERDE (who should be in brown, but played by the same actor as plays the priest) enters stage right with a Bible.

BEARERS: We have brought you the Sun.
We have brought you the summer.

FRIAR DE VALVERDE: I don't want to hear your blasphemies! Uncover him! Let me see the face of the Devil!

BEARERS: We have brought you the Sun. We have brought you the summer.

FRIAR DE VALVERDE: In the name of the Pope and the King of Spain show me this creature! Or is your litter empty?

The curtains are pulled back and the INCA ATAHUALLPA steps out. FRIAR DE VALVERDE holds out a hand as if to keep the INCA in the litter.

Back, Satan! Do not stand upright like a man of good heart! Your empire is confiscated by the Holy Catholic Church and his Catholic Majesty of Spain! I demand that you be baptized and abjure your ancient evil faith! Accept Christ and be humble!

FRIAR DE VALVERDE thrusts the Bible into the INCA's hands.

Say after me, with your hand on this holy book... I swear to agree to the annexation of my empire to that of the Spanish king, and the souls of my people to the Church of Rome...

The INCA throws the book down.

INCA: Are you so simple? You stand in the midst of my country and talk like a child and expect me to listen? Where is the man I came to see?

FRIAR DE VALVERDE: (*To PIZARRO.*) We are wasting our breath talking to this dog, full of pride as he is.

PIZARRO waves a white scarf. Blackout. Cannon. Gunfire. Confusion. In the darkness PIZARRO can be heard shouting.

PIZARRO: Lunge! Detach! Lunge! Detach! Lunge! Detach!

Lights up. The BEARERS are in a heap. The INCA in chains. PIZARRO gets in the litter and the two CONQUISTADORS carry him off, the INCA following behind like a roped horse.

GENERAL CROOK: The Incas failed because they had forgotten the use of arms. One-hundred-and-seventeen Spaniards against five million Incas! What odds!

CRAZY HORSE: Treachery is a great ally, Gray Wolf. The white man from the East always had that regiment on his side. How do you fight ambition? How do you defeat greed? How do you turn the flank of deceit or charge the lie? Treachery is an army of millions! The cold, calculating heart is a fortress that no cannon can breach.

GENERAL CROOK: Soon the wealth of Peru was flooding back across the Atlantic to Spain to support her continental empire. Spain had become the most powerful nation on earth. The gold of America bought her the fear of the civilised world.

CRAZY HORSE: And the New World
Was made old
by gold.

GENERAL CROOK about-turns, salutes the flag, then marches off right. CRAZY HORSE sits by the BEARERS and starts to sing a morning-song.

The People, where are the People?
Where are the Tainos now?
Where are the Arawaks?

Where are the Aztecs?
Where are the Incas?
The People, where are the People?

Light darken. The wind rises. The huddled, blanketed figures enter from the rear of the auditorium. The BEARERS slowly rise. They all join CRAZY HORSE in the chant, louder and louder. The people are everywhere in the theatre, singing.

The People, where are the People?
Where are the Tainos now?
Where are the Arawaks?
Where are the Aztecs?
Where are the Incas?
The People, where are the People?

The moon is illuminated. As the chant continues, over and over, GENERAL CROOK enters with a bucket of whitewash and a brush and carefully paints in the Caribbean, Mexico, Honduras, Peru. The paint should run into the adjoining countries. When he has finished he exits and THE PEOPLE fade away, leaving the auditorium empty.

End of Act One.

ACT TWO

Thudding of a drum. Bugle call. Enter GENERAL CROOK and CRAZY HORSE to their places. The pianist plays a selected piece by Claude le Jeune (or another French composer of the period). After a bar, the Fleur-de-Lys is carried in from the rear of the auditorium by JACQUES CARTIER. He marches down the aisle, stabs at the St Lawrence valley, plants the flag.

CARTIER: Here! I claim these lands on behalf of King Francis the First of France.

CRAZY HORSE: The Iroquois held that land from the Master of Life. It was theirs.

The pianist plays a selected piece by William Byrd. The Royal Standard of Elizabeth I is carried down the aisle by SIR WALTER RALEIGH. He prods the coast of South Carolina, plants the flag.

SIR WALTER RALEIGH: Here! I claim these lands on behalf of Queen Elizabeth of England!

CRAZY HORSE: The Santee Sioux held that land from the Great Spirit. It was theirs.

The pianist plays a selected piece by Sweelinck (or any other Dutch composer of the early seventeenth century), and the flag of the Netherlands is carried in by PETER MINUIT. He points at Manhattan Island, plants the flag.

PETER MINUIT: Here! I claim these lands on behalf of the States General and the Dutch West India Company!

CRAZY HORSE: But here it wasn't so easy. A passing band of Indians overheard...

TWO INDIANS (the tribe is not known) appear from behind the map of America. They wag their fingers at PETER MINUIT, then hold out their hands.

FIRST INDIAN: One hundred dollars.

PETER MINUIT: I'll give you five!

SECOND INDIAN: Seventy dollars!

PETER MINUIT: I'll give you ten!

FIRST INDIAN: Fifty dollars!

PETER MINUIT: I'll give you fifteen!

SECOND INDIAN: Forty dollars!

PETER MINUIT: I'll give you twenty!

The TWO INDIANS nod. They all shake hands. PETER MINUIT produces a piece of parchment and a pen. He spreads it out on the floor. The TWO INDIANS start singing and dance all over the paper. PETER MINUIT shoves them off and waves the pen under their noses.

Sign! Sign!

FIRST INDIAN takes the quill off MINUIT, looks at it, then sticks it in his hair and carries on dancing. MINUIT grabs the quill and bends down over the parchment, showing them how to sign. The TWO INDIANS play leapfrog over his back.

Sign! Sign, you damned savages!

The TWO INDIANS kneel down by MINUIT's side. He gives the FIRST INDIAN the quill. FIRST INDIAN gives it to SECOND INDIAN, who gives it back again. MINUIT gives it to SECOND INDIAN, who gives it to FIRST INDIAN, who gives it back again. Then both INDIANS put their hands together and pray.

FIRST INDIAN: O Great Spirit, guide our hands!

SECOND INDIAN: For we cannot write!

MINUIT: Then make your mark!

The TWO INDIANS make their marks, shake hands with
MINUIT, receive their twenty dollars in coin.

MINUIT: That's settled that! Now the island is mine. Not
bad for twenty dollars, eh?

FIRST INDIAN: You got a bargain.

SECOND INDIAN: But now we must be going home.

MINUIT: Wait a minute. You can't live here any more.
This place is mine.

FIRST INDIAN: We never lived here in the first place. We
are just passing through.

The TWO INDIANS run off. MINUIT chases them, then comes back,
takes up the parchment as if to tear it, pauses, shrugs, then rolls it up
and puts it back in his shirt.

MINUIT: It will have to do.

GENERAL CROOK: And thus began the legend of the
'Honest Injun'.

The three Colonisers – French, English and Dutch – stand
with their flags. Sounds of wind, sea, the screams of gulls.
Enter three groups through the auditorium, carrying poles on
which sails are raised (in the way a trade union banner is
carried).

The Atlantic Ocean was bridged more often than the
Seine, the Thames or the Zuyder Zee.

CRAZY HORSE: And they brought a different god, for
they were rebels against the Spanish way. There was no
talk of the great chief in Rome. Their god was in a book
and they brought him in libraries of Bibles, they sailed
on Bibles...

GENERAL CROOK: Puritans from England, Huguenots
from France, Calvinists from the Netherlands, they came

to plant the orchards of their faith as well as their apples. Europe was once again in the hands of Rome and they went to America, preferring a devil they did not know to a devil they knew.

The three ships sail slowly towards the upper level. The EMIGRANTS pray together in a spoken chorus.

EMIGRANTS: Sail with us, O Lord,
    For you were a sailor,
    You walked upon the water
    As these wooden shoes of ships
    Tread the waves:
    Protect us from the unknown
    Depths of this mighty sea,
    Protect us from the heathen
    And the ways of darkness,
    And on land, as on sea,
    Keep us close to Thee.
    Amen. Amen. Amen.

The ships reach the upper level. The EMIGRANTS land, carrying axes, ropes, guns, spades. They cluster round the flags. Sound effects of axes biting into wood, trees crashing, spades turning earth. The EMIGRANTS mime with the sounds, building, building, working, working. The sounds get louder and louder, the EMIGRANTS work faster and faster until the sound is deafening and the EMIGRANTS are moving at frenzied speed. The INDIANS enter on the upper level and watch, shaking their heads in wonder. They carry baskets of fruit, corn, vegetables. The EMIGRANTS work on. The TWO INDIANS shrug and go out, leaving the baskets behind. Sounds stop abruptly. The EMIGRANTS drop to the ground with exhaustion and sleep. Lights down. Night.

GENERAL CROOK: Their god was work, their Christ, industry. For a man to pay his way in the world was salvation started. They bored into America like beetles.

CRAZY HORSE: They felled our forests, polluted our streams, slew our game and scorned our ways. Like fools, the Indian gave the beetle food, helped him with his burrowing.

Sound of feet marching, tramping, hundreds of boots, an army, tramp! tramp! As the moon shines on and the EMIGRANTS sleep, the tramping grows louder. At its zenith, there is a loud yell, the lights go up and METACOMET, Chief of the Wampanoags, leaps onstage in full war-paint, armed, wearing a golden crown.

METACOMET: Enough, Yinglees! Enough Yinglees! Out! Out! Damn Yankees!

The FLAG-BEARERS and the EMIGRANTS retreat to the lower level in confusion. The Dutch and French flags are placed alongside the Stars and Stripes, the English remains. METACOMET takes the crown off and throws it into the midst of the EMIGRANTS.

Take this hat away you gave me! Tell the White Father over the Eastern Sea that it is heavy and hollow…

FIRST EMIGRANT: But, King Philip…

METACOMET: You flatter me with an empty title! You duped my father into thinking that he ruled his own house while it was you who governed my people! I am not a king! Nor is your king a king here! You are going home, back to where you came from!

Enter four WAMPANOAGS in full war-paint with bows. They line up behind METACOMET.

Go away! Go back to England! Take your god, your books, and your guns and go! We had peace in this land until the Trickster spirits brought you to torment us! Metacomet speaks! Out! Out!

The EMIGRANTS murmur and brace themselves into a line. The WAMPANOAGS mime the firing of arrows, the EMIGRANTS mime the firing of guns. Slowly the EMIGRANTS advance, the WAMPANOAGS drop one by one until only METACOMET is left. Pause. METACOMET backs away, faced by the hostile eyes of the EMIGRANTS.

Where is King Philip now? Where is your slave?

He throws himself at the EMIGRANTS. They seize him and he goes down under a milling heap of fists and boots. Blackout. Two spots on GENERAL CROOK and CRAZY HORSE. The stage is cleared. The English flag is put with the Stars and Stripes.

GENERAL CROOK: In a campaign remarkable for its ferocity, King Philip was defeated. The settlers looked upon his attempt to drive them out of their homes as a betrayal. Had the Indian not been baptized, educated in an English school?

CRAZY HORSE: Metacomet had the right idea. He was the first Indian chief to see the danger and the first to try and create an alliance against the whites. He brought the Narragansets of Rhode Island, the Pequots of Connecticut, and other small tribes into a common cause against the invaders. He saw the way to beat them back into the sea.

GENERAL CROOK: King Philip lost his war. He was caught and hacked to bits and his wife and child sold into slavery. He had been outgunned and outgeneralled.

CRAZY HORSE: And the tribes of the alliance perished. They were no more, like snow in summer. Now we can add to my song.

A drum starts up, soft rattle, CRAZY HORSE takes up his chant again.

The People, where are the People?
Where are the Tainos now?
Where are the Arawaks?
Where are the Aztecs?
Where are the Incas?
Where are the Wampanoags?
Where are the Pequots?
Where are the Narragansets?
Where are the People?

GENERAL CROOK: (*Pointing with his sabre on the map.*)
For the next two centuries the European colonists moved
inland through the passes of the Allegheny Mountains
and down the westward-flowing rivers of the Mississippi...

CRAZY HORSE: (*Bitterly.*) The Great Waters!

GENERAL CROOK: And then up the Missouri...

CRAZY HORSE: The Great Muddy!

GENERAL CROOK: Various chiefs tried to do what King
Philip...

CRAZY HORSE: The hero Metacomet!

GENERAL CROOK: ...had tried to do. Pontiac of the
Ottawas united the tribes of the Great Lakes to drive the
British back over the Allegheny Mountains in 1760. He
failed because he made a fatal error – he brought the
French into the alliance – there was war in Europe...the
British and the French...

CRAZY HORSE: There was always war in Europe!

GENERAL CROOK: And the French broke faith with the
peaux-rouges, their Indian allies, at the siege of Detroit.
The Ottawas were crushed.

CRAZY HORSE: Where are the Ottawas? Trusting a white
man? What innocence!

GENERAL CROOK: Fifty years later Tecumseh of the Shawnees formed a confederacy of mid-western tribes to protect their homelands from the British, Dutch, French, German, Spanish invaders. The Scramble for America was on!

CRAZY HORSE: Tecumseh died in battle, his dream died with him.

GENERAL CROOK: For the first half of the nineteenth century the Miamis of the fertile Ohio valley fought battle after battle…

CRAZY HORSE: Signed treaty after treaty…

GENERAL CROOK: Until there was nothing left of their land to cede.

CRAZY HORSE: Miami, Miami…do you know the word?

GENERAL CROOK: Black Hawk of the Foxes refused to hand over his tribal lands to the white settlers after the white man's war of 1812, when the Americans fought the –

CRAZY HORSE: Notice the name – Americans! Americans! We were the Americans.

GENERAL CROOK: By then the Revolution of 1776 was ancient history, Crazy Horse! We licked the British hands down, all ways up! We declared our independence…

CRAZY HORSE: Yes, your independence! What about ours? We were the first Americans! We had a right to be consulted!

GENERAL CROOK: Let's get back to Black Hawk. He was quite a soldier.

CRAZY HORSE: America arrived without the Red Indian even knowing about it. Out of the white men's wars came a paper, a name, another army. The United States. Europe was inside us.

GENERAL CROOK stands to attention and salutes. The pianist plays 'The Stars and Stripes'. CRAZY HORSE holds his head in his hands.

And then they started stirring the pot again. They had sold The People into slavery for two hundred years, now they went to Africa and bought slaves to bring to America – black slaves, for they were fast running out of red as blood runs out of an opened vein.

Slow fade to darkness. Chinking of chains. Blackout. Chinking of chains becomes rhythmical as the voices of the SLAVES sing the slave-song.

SLAVES: You cannot see us
    because of the darkness,
    you cannot hold us
    because of the night,
    we are black in the blackness
    and blue in the blueness
    of the sea and the bruise
    in our hearts.
    Hahe! (*The chains crash.*) Hahe!
    Only Death sets us free!

Sounds of the ship again, creaking of timbers, stretching of yards. The chinking of chains continues in rhythm. Blackout continues, complete darkness.

We are sold to work sugar,
we are sold to work cotton,
we are sold to be horses
and our manhood forgotten!
We die on the coast,
we die in the hold,
we live to be bought
with American gold!

Hahe! (*The chains crash.*) Hahe!
Only death sets us free.

Ships' sounds fade. Hammering on a block. Murmur of a crowd. Blackout remains.

AUCTIONEER: Now what am I bid?

SLAVES: I'm ten! I'm five! I'm twelve! I'm alive. Bid in dollars or gold, I'm here to be sold!

Crash of the AUCTIONEER's hammer.

GENERAL CROOK: The Indian would not work! He had never learned to work! The routine of your lives was idleness!

CRAZY HORSE: They brought the black men in thousands to work the fields of a plant that could not be eaten.

GENERAL CROOK: Cotton, the mainstay of the American export trade with the Old Country.

CRAZY HORSE: We were being conquered by the price of a thin shirt. Where the black men came in, we were pushed out...

GENERAL CROOK: We were a young, vigorous, expanding country. We needed room! People came to America for a new life, to be free to live in peace, to worship the god of their choice...

CRAZY HORSE: Gold.

GENERAL CROOK: Dammit, Crazy Horse, gold to the white man was only a means to an end. Our economy was based on gold. We had to have it.

Enter stage left the FRENCH ESTATE AGENT. He is dressed in top hat, coat and breeches and carries a cane.

FRENCH ESTATE AGENT: M'sieur! Psst! Psst! A word in your ear!

GENERAL CROOK: Who's this goddamned dandy?

FRENCH ESTATE AGENT: (*Sidling over to CROOK.*) 'Ere, 'ow would you like to buy a piece of America? You like?

The FRENCH ESTATE AGENT takes out a sheaf of postcards and sticks them under CROOK's nose.

Voila! Is she not lovely?

GENERAL CROOK: That's New Orleans! What the hell's going on here?

FRENCH ESTATE AGENT: 'Ere is the Mississippi, the Red River, is Louisiana not beautiful, eh? You can have 'er, for the right price, of course. You like what you see?

CRAZY HORSE: Ask him about sitting tenants.

GENERAL CROOK: (*To FRENCH ESTATE AGENT.*) You heard him. What about sitting tenants?

FRENCH ESTATE AGENT: Take no notice of 'im. He is a peau-rouge. Listen, my friend, the French people are willing to sell you this desirable property with magnificent views over the Gulf of Mexico for a mere fifteen million dollars –

CRAZY HORSE: Ask him about the chattels, then. Do they go with the property? Do you get the Chitimichas, the Taenzas, the Natchez, the Karoks, the Yazoos, the Choctaws and the Chickasaws thrown in?

GENERAL CROOK: Well, Crazy Horse, it sounds a bargain. It's a better way of acquiring territory than war. (*To the FRENCH ESTATE AGENT.*) I reckon if you go and see the President in Washington he'll be interested.

FRENCH ESTATE AGENT: Merci bien. Au revoir.

The FRENCH ESTATE AGENT exits after a courtly bow and a wave of his stick.

CRAZY HORSE: And that is how it was done. The white man had come to America for gold, he got gold, and with that gold he now started buying the land off people who didn't even own it. The earth was bought and sold from under The People's feet. In 1803 the Great White Father bought Louisiana.

Enter stage left a MEXICAN GENERAL. He is in military uniform and so loaded with medals that he leans over to one side.

MEXICAN GENERAL: Hey, damn Yankee, c'm 'ere, I gotta someting to tell you.

GENERAL CROOK: What do you want, you damn greaser?

MEXICAN GENERAL: Now we don' like da war, eh? What is da point of it all? We are neighbours. Now, I'll do you a deal, a nice deal. The Mexican government, well, we don' wanna get in your hairs, eh? Like you say, we like to keep it peaceful.

GENERAL CROOK: Speak up then, Mex. We've trounced you all over the place lately. What's the deal?

MEXICAN GENERAL: You remember the deal you did with the Spanish government in 1813?

GENERAL CROOK: Yes, we bought West Florida from them after the war.

CRAZY HORSE: The squatters at that time were the Bilox, the Seminoles, the Apalachee. What rights had they got in these dealings? They had only lived there for ten thousand years.

MEXICAN GENERAL: Well, if I remember right, you paid five million dollars for that piece of land.

GENERAL CROOK: That's right.

MEXICAN GENERAL: How much you give for California, Utah, Texas and New Mexico?

Pause. GENERAL CROOK scratches his head.

GENERAL CROOK: Dammit, man, that's a mighty big parcel of territory.

CRAZY HORSE: (*Angrily facing the MEXICAN GENERAL.*) Who says you can sell this land? It is not yours to sell!

MEXICAN GENERAL: Who is this barbarian? Get back to your reservation, Indios!

CRAZY HORSE: You brought your wars to our land and you sought to settle them with our land and our gold. Who are you to put the earth on the market? Are you God? You have enough medals for God but inside you are a cheap swindler. You cannot sell what is not yours!

MEXICAN GENERAL: Yankee, don't listen to this ignorant savage. He is talking nonsense. You and me are men of the world, eh? What will you offer me? These places are like Paradise on earth.

CRAZY HORSE: What about the Apaches?

MEXICAN GENERAL: Apaches! (*Spits on the ground.*) Fiends from Hell! They are no better than rattlesnake! The gringos can have the Apaches and the Modocs, the Mohaves, the Paiutes, the Shastas, the Yumas, the Navahoes and the Utes. Because of this little disadvantage I am only asking for fifteen million dollars. Without the Indians, well, I think I ask for twenty-five millions.

GENERAL CROOK: That's a fair offer, Mex. If I was you I'd go and have a talk with the President. I know he thinks that we should get our border down on to the Rio Grande.

The MEXICAN GENERAL salutes, then exits. CRAZY HORSE returns to his alcove and squats on his blanket.

In 1844 the Mexican government sold Texas, California, Utah and New Mexico to the United States for fifteen million dollars. We were across to the West coast!

GENERAL CROOK marches off and gets the whitewash and brush. He paints in all the territory west of 95° longitude, then sweeps round through Texas, New Mexico, to Utah as CRAZY HORSE sings his mourning song, accompanied by drum and rattles.

CRAZY HORSE: Where are the People?
Where are the Chitimichas?
Where are the Taenzas?
Where are the Natchez?
Where are the Karoks?
Where are the Yazoos?
Where are the Choctaws?
Where are the Chickasaws?
Where are the Bilox?
Where are the Apalachees?
Where are the Seminoles?
Where are the Apaches?
Where are the Modocs?
Where are the Mohaves?
Where are the Paiutes?
Where are the Shastas?
Where are the Yumas?
Where are the Navahoes?
Where are the Utes?

GENERAL CROOK puts away the whitewash and returns to his alcove. CRAZY HORSE sits with his head in his hands.

Remember Sharp Knife? (*Stands up and goes to map.*)

GENERAL CROOK: You mean Andrew Jackson? A damn fine soldier, and President of the United States…

CRAZY HORSE: As well as the killer of thousands of Cherokees, Chickasaws, Choctaws, Creeks and Seminoles.

GENERAL CROOK: Dammit, man, he was a soldier. He fought you Indians because it was his duty.

CRAZY HORSE: A soldier is a man of honour?

GENERAL CROOK: His honour is his life.

CRAZY HORSE: Then why did Sharp Knife say in 1829 that this was the Permanent Indian Frontier? This line, the course of the Great Waters, the Mississippi, was to be the wall I wanted. Beyond it no white man could go. That was the law he made through your Congress. It was written down! He promised that we should have all this land in the West for ourselves. And we – fools that we were – believed him!

GENERAL CROOK: The war with Mexico changed everything. The settlers were pouring into Wisconsin and Iowa, the miners were in Utah where gold had been found. Jackson couldn't hold them back.

CRAZY HORSE: Then do not talk to me of laws and peace! Sharp Knife allowed his white children to break all the rules and they were never punished. Only the Indians died.

GENERAL CROOK: Minnesota became a state, its frontier extending a hundred miles beyond the *second* Permanent Indian Frontier.

CRAZY HORSE: The People were in a vice and only war could save them.

The pianist softly plays 'Way Down South in Dixie'. The tune is taken up by whistling. A vaulting horse is dragged on stage (to the lower level). GENERAL CROOK mounts his steed. The AUCTIONEER and the NEGRO go out. The pianist slides into 'The Battle Hymn of the Republic'. Softly, slowly, he plays as GENERAL CROOK begins to trot, breaks into a canter, then he thunders fortissimo as GENERAL CROOK draws his sabre and...

GENERAL CROOK: Charge! Long live the Union!

Lights switch to red. GENERAL CROOK slows down, he cuts and thrusts with his sabre in slow motion. The pianist picks out both the Confederate and Union tunes alternately, then fades. GENERAL CROOK is exhausted, slides off his horse and pushes it into his alcove.

CRAZY HORSE: The war that The People thought might save them was a white man's war – the North versus the South. The white men forgot the red men and fought over the black men. It was the worst war ever seen in America. When we saw how the white man fought his friends we knew what we could expect as his enemies. And his armies got bigger and bigger, his wagon-guns longer, his pony soldiers as numerous as summer flies.

GENERAL CROOK: The United States were preserved. We whipped the rebels and on July 28th, 1868 the Fourteenth Amendment became part of the Constitution. All citizens of the United States were to have equal rights, black or white...

CRAZY HORSE: But not red. The Civil War had not been fought for us.

The red light fades and is replaced by the moon. From every entrance, stage and auditorium, steps an Indian in full war paint. They are CHIEFS of the people who fought the United States Army from 1860 to 1890. The stand round the stage

and auditorium and step a pace forward as CRAZY HORSE
calls out their names.

These are only the leaders of The People in those last
thirty years. By the time the whites had shut the door of
Freedom in our faces, The People had been cut in half.
We were not many, maybe three hundred thousand of us
were left. We wanted peace but we were not ready to take
the black man's place. We were men! We were The
People!
Little Crow of the Santee Sioux
Black Kettle of the Southern Cheyennes
Mangas Colorado of the Mimbrenos Apaches
Spotted Tail of the Brulés
Satanta of the Kiowas
Quanah Parker of the Comanches
Captain Jack of the Modocs
Joseph of the Nez Percés
Big Foot of the Minneconjous
Standing Bear of the Poncas
Sitting Bull of the Hunkpapa Sioux
Wovoka of the Paiutes

Pause.

and Crazy Horse, the Big Dreamer.
(*To the audience.*) You are now in a familiar situation. You
are surrounded by Indians!

All the CHIEFS leap in the air and shout. It must be a
clear, sudden sound. Pause.

Since the time when I was a boy in the Black Hills I have
been a dreamer, a seeker after visions. This was never
the real world to me. Even in life I sought after the
dream. I went up into the mountains, I lay on rafts of
wood on hidden lakes for days without food, I sat under
the stars, always I stayed with my dream. Crazy Horse,
the Big Dreamer, was the dream of The People. I had

seen it all from long ago. From the time we crossed the land-bridge to this moment, I was in the head of the Great Spirit, peering from behind his eyes. I saw what would happen to The People but all I had was my short life, my lance and my horse, to fight against the whites and what they were doing. By being born I became just one Indian and I faced a truth as terrible as my dream. My dream and the truth were the same thing. (*Pause.*) MOUNT UP, GENERAL GRAY WOLF THREE STARS GOD ALMIGHTY!

CRAZY HORSE runs to the vaulting horse and drags it out to the centre of the lower level, pats the leather. As soon as he touches the leather, the CHIEFS scream again and rush towards GENERAL CROOK, lift him up and dump him on the vaulting-horse. There should be a moment of nervousness as the CHIEFS descend on the GENERAL, then relief as he is hoisted into the air.

Now be all our enemies, Gray Wolf!

LITTLE CROW: Be Myrick the trader who told us to eat grass!

BLACK KETTLE: Be Colonel Chivington who killed us at Sand Creek!

MANGAS COLORADO: Be Colonel West who broke his word!

SPOTTED TAIL: Be the white hunters who slaughtered the buffalo!

SATANTA: Be General Sheridan who wanted us dead!

QUANAH PARKER: Be Great Warrior Sherman who butchered our horses!

CAPTAIN JACK: Be Commissioner Meacham who told us the Law was dead!

JOSEPH: Be One-Armed Soldier Howard who drove us to the ground!

BIG FOOT: Be Colonel Forsyth who killed us in the snow!

STANDING BEAR: Be Inspector Kemble who took us to the Quapaw to die!

SITTING BULL: Be Hard Backsides Custer who tried to break our hearts!

WOVOKA: Be white! Be white!

CRAZY HORSE: Be yourself who came looking for me in the Cold Moons! Hopo hook-ahay! And be the Great White Father in Washington who turned his back upon his children. Let's go!

The pianist plays a steady, monotonous rhythm of heavy bass chords. Drummers occupy CRAZY HORSE's alcove and take up the rhythm. The CHIEFS return to their previous positions around stage and auditorium step by step to the rhythm. GENERAL CROOK sits astride his horse, looking straight ahead. The pianist hits the chords again. The drummers drum. LITTLE CROW comes forward.

LITTLE CROW: It was my fault. I had signed the treaties that tricked away our land around the Minnesota River. All we had left was a strip by the waters and the whites were waiting for that. The Santee Sioux were poor. The Santee Sioux were hungry. All we had was our money and our rations from the Great Council in Washington, but in that year they had no money, for the gold was being spent on the war between the Bluecoats and the Graycoats. My people were starving. The rations were in the stores but there was no money. We saw food but could not eat. I went to the trader Myrick... (*He looks up at GENERAL CROOK.*) and I said, 'We have waited a long time. Give us food so we do not starve. When the money comes it will be yours.' What did he say?

GENERAL CROOK: So far as I'm concerned, if they are hungry let them eat grass or their own dung.

Pause. Then GENERAL CROOK slowly slides off his horse and lies down, his mouth open. LITTLE CROW takes a handful of grass out of his shirt and stuffs it into CROOK's mouth.

LITTLE CROW: So we made Myrick eat grass himself. Then we fought the soldiers who came. We fought as men and it was the guns that beat us. When we were taken they put us in prison and tried us. The Great White Father Lincoln said thirty-nine of us must hang and hang we did. Those that were left were put in ships to go up the Missouri River to where the soil was barren, there was no game, and the alkaline water unfit for drinking. The Santee Sioux were finished.

GENERAL CROOK spits out the grass and remounts his horse. LITTLE CROW shakes his head and returns to his place. The pianist strikes the chords again, the drummers drum. BLACK KETTLE comes into the spot.

BLACK KETTLE: I am Cheyenne and I could talk of massacre and murder, of land stealing, of the long walks of my people through hard winters to find a refuge from the pony-soldiers. But I will not. My story will be one story. It will show you that we were not perfect, we were proud. Two boys, Chief-in-Head and Humped Over, killed a white man who wrongly accused them of stealing a cow. One cow…

Enter CHIEF-IN-HEAD, stage right, and HUMPED OVER, stage left. CHIEF-IN-HEAD wears a full eagle-feather war-bonnet, HUMPED OVER a single feather. They enter and stand still.

The Army came to the Cheyennes and demanded these murderers. We did not want war, we were sick of war, but we could not hand over the boys. They had gone to the Wolf Mountains. They said that the white man had deserved to die. Their fathers went to them and asked that they come down to the soldiers. They would give them a fair trial. The boys laughed and said:

CHIEF-IN-HEAD: We have heard of the fair trials. We will not come in.

HUMPED OVER: But tomorrow at noon we will be at this point in the hills.

CHIEF-IN-HEAD: Tell the soldiers to come and get us.

BLACK KETTLE: That night we danced for the boys. We sent them two of our best horses, our richest shirts, our finest arms. The boys painted themselves as for the old Sun Dance which the Great Father in Washington had forbidden us to perform, they anointed themselves with oil, and then waited in the noonday sun.

CHIEF-IN-HEAD and HUMPED OVER should dress and paint themselves as BLACK KETTLE speaks, following the course of the dialogue.

(*To CROOK.*) Sir, you are two hundred mounted men. The Army of the Great Father sent out three troops of pony soldiers to catch our boys. Ride!

CROOK salutes, rides, bugle call.

GENERAL CROOK: Forward!

BLACK KETTLE: The pony soldiers came to the point in the hills. Here the earth was like a bowl and The People were there, all of us, old and young, to see what our boys would do. We heard their singing and knew the sound of it.

CHIEF-IN-HEAD: I will stop growing older.
They will put an end
To my growing!

HUMPED OVER: Watch us while we are riding,
How we ride our horses.
Watch our skill.

CROOK reins in, then dismounts, takes out his revolver and stands behind the horse, facing the upper level. The BOYS carry on chanting, then bring down their lances and charge at CROOK, miming the horses beneath them. Sound of heavy rifle-fire. The BOYS chant on. CROOK mimes blazing away at his attackers. HUMPED OVER drops. CHIEF-IN-HEAD gets closer, carries through past CROOK and then drops.

BLACK KETTLE: Chief-In-Head took six wounds. He rode through the two hundred men dead, but still on his horse. Humped Over was not hit bad and crawled to cover in a dry wash. The soldiers came for him and he fought well.

GENERAL CROOK: (*Turning to the audience, for the first time evidently moved by what has happened.*) A young lieutenant found him. These are his words: 'Crawling through the brush towards him, we suddenly discovered him dead, and we were most startled at the weird beauty of the picture he made as he lay in his vivid colour of costume and painted face, his red blood dyeing the yellow of autumn leaves on which he fell.'

BLACK KETTLE: That is my story.

BLACK KETTLE returns to his place. CHIEF-IN-HEAD and HUMPED OVER go out. MANGAS COLORADO jumps into the spot. Throughout his account of his betrayal and death he mimes the action, instructing CROOK when he requires his help in telling the story. CROOK obeys like an automaton, showing no feeling, his expression frozen. He becomes each antagonist for each CHIEF as they tell their mimed stories. Every CHIEF addresses the audience throughout.

MANGAS COLORADO: My people lived in Arizona and New Mexico, from the Chiricuhua Mountains to the Mogollons. We tried to stop the white men coming. In the war between the Bluecoats and the Graycoats we managed to drive the Graycoats out into the East. Then came Star Chief Carleton from California along the old trail through our mountains. We fought him, and he suffered at our hands. So they asked for a truce. Colonel Joseph West (*CROOK salutes.*) met me at Fort McLean. He made me a prisoner although I had come under the white flag. That night he told two soldiers to guard me. He said to them…

GENERAL CROOK: I want him dead or alive tomorrow morning, do you understand, I want him dead.

MANGAS COLORADO: I lay down to sleep by the fire under my blanket. The soldiers heated their bayonets in the fire and put them to the soles of my feet. I endured it until I could take no more, then I rose and said, 'I am no child to be played with in this way.' The soldiers pointed their muskets at me and shot me dead.

Pause. MANGAS COLORADO looks up at GENERAL CROOK, who stares straight ahead. Shaking his head MANGAS COLORADO returns to his place. CROOK sits still on his horse, his head hanging. The pianist plays the chords, the drummers drum. SATANTA, SPOTTED TAIL and QUANAH PARKER jump forward into the spot.

SATANTA: This is how we hunted buffalo, the big ones.

Sound effect of cattle lowing and bellowing (a substitute for buffalo noise). The BUFFALO enters from rear of auditorium. The four CHIEFS are armed with lances. The piano stops and the drums get louder as the four CHIEFS hunt the BUFFALO, two on either side, keeping the BUFFALO on a straight course. The CHIEFS shout at the BUFFALO. As the hunt progresses round the theatre, the remaining CHIEFS sing and clap.

CHIEFS: Ha-hey-ya-hey
ya-hey-ya-hey-ya-hey
ha-hey-ya-hey
ya-hey-ya-hey-ya-hey
ha-hey-ya-he
ya-hey-ya-hey-ya-hey
ha-hey-ya-he.

The BUFFALO is killed by a lance thrust to the heart.

SATANTA: (*Suddenly turning on CROOK.*) You butcher!
Your belly never needed that much meat!

QUANAH PARKER: In one year the whites killed four
million buffalo.

SPOTTED TAIL: They killed more buffalo than Indians.
They put all their heart into it. They killed for the coat,
for the coat!

SATANTA: Now you are Sheridan, I ask you – sir, should
not something be done to stop the senseless killing of the
buffalo? What is your answer, General? What will you
do about the white hunters?

GENERAL CROOK: Let them kill, skin and sell until the
buffalo is exterminated, as it is the only way to bring
lasting peace and allow civilisation to advance.

SATANTA: Starve us to death. Take the meat out of the
mother's mouth. You are children murdering children.
Death is the white man's game.

*CAPTAIN JACK leaps out into the spot, shaking his fist
under CROOK's nose.*

CAPTAIN JACK: Councils! Councils! Councils! Oh,
councils killed poor Captain Jack! In our valley there
ran enough deer, antelope, duck and fish for everyone!
And where did I end up?

SATANTA, QUANAH PARKER, SPOTTED TAIL leave the spot, dragging the buffalo. CAPTAIN JACK continues. He is slightly mad, very active and full of gestures.

CAPTAIN JACK: Hear me! This man Canby here has killed me! I charge him!

GENERAL CROOK: My orders are to move you out of the Lost River Valley by force if need be.

CAPTAIN JACK: (*Grovelling, in caricature.*) I will go I will take all my people with me. Let me kiss your boots!

GENERAL CROOK: (*Kicking at CAPTAIN JACK.*) I'm not here to make trouble, Captain Jack.

CAPTAIN JACK: You would never make trouble. Cheat us out of our land, yes. Kill our people, yes. Set fire to our village, yes. But trouble? Never. (*He clings to GENERAL CROOK's boots, smothering them with kisses.*)

GENERAL CROOK: Off, you red devil!

CAPTAIN JACK springs back, his manner changed.

CAPTAIN JACK: Then we saw that we were men. We went to a place where no man can live, the Lava Beds, where there is nothing but stone. No grass grows. No birds sing. It is the grave. We fought the soldiers there and they killed me. The Modocs were finished. But I had words to say.

CAPTAIN JACK runs from place to place, delivering a sentence at one place, running, pausing, delivering another. He does this at top speed. GENERAL CROOK has to strain round to keep him in view.

I am but one man. (*Move.*)
I am the voice of my people. (*Move.*)
I am not afraid to die. (*Move.*)
I have come to these rocks to fight. (*Move.*)

I have a red skin. (*Move.*)
I have red blood. (*Move.*)
I have one heart. (*Move.*)

CAPTAIN JACK stands still, pointing at his heart. CROOK raises his revolver and shoots him. CAPTAIN JACK holds his heart and skips back to his place among the chiefs.

(*Shaking his fist.*) Even the stones you wanted, even the stones!

The pianist strikes up the chords, the drummers drum. Old CHIEF JOSEPH walks into the spot and stands in front of GENERAL CROOK, then he mimes walking.

JOSEPH: General One-Armed Howard, why are you following me?

GENERAL CROOK: The President has ordered that you move out of Wallowa Valley.

JOSEPH: But two years ago the Great White Father promised the Nez Percés this land for ever.

GENERAL CROOK: He cannot control the settlers. They come and they come.

JOSEPH: But he can control the Indians? Are we better children?

GENERAL CROOK: The government has set aside a reservation and you must go in it.

JOSEPH: The land is part of our bodies. We never give up the earth, for it would be like giving up ourselves.

GENERAL CROOK: I don't want to offend your religion but you must talk about practical things. Twenty times over I hear that the earth is your mother and about chieftainship from the earth. I want to hear no more but to come to business at once.

JOSEPH: Who can tell me what I must do in my own country?

GENERAL CROOK spurs his horse on. JOSEPH starts to run (on the spot).

GENERAL CROOK: You have thirty days to move!

JOSEPH: Why are you in such a hurry? I cannot get my people ready in that time. The Snake River is very high and our stock is scattered…

JOSEPH slows down to a walk.

GENERAL CROOK: (*Prodding JOSEPH with his toe.*) Listen, you red bastard, if you let the time run over by one day the soldiers will be there to drive you on to the reservation and all your cattle and horses left outside will fall into the hands of the white men!

JOSEPH starts to run again.

JOSEPH: So I led my people into the Bitterroot Mountains. We were going to run for Canada. The soldiers followed. We ran and we ran and we ran. They caught us and killed us, then we ran again, we ran through the winter.

GENERAL CROOK gallops after JOSEPH, waving his sabre.

GENERAL CROOK: Come back! Come back! The Great White Father commands!

JOSEPH: Then came the time when there was no more running in us. We were spent.

JOSEPH falls to the ground. GENERAL CROOK looks down on him from his horse.

GENERAL CROOK: If you will give up your arms I will spare your lives and send you to your reservation. I am not a hard man.

JOSEPH: General Howard, I know your heart. What you told me before I have in my heart. Our chiefs are killed. The old men are all dead. It is cold and we have no blankets. The little children are freezing to death. I am tired, my heart is sick and sad. From where the sun now stands I will fight no more for ever.

Pause. GENERAL CROOK slumps forward on his horse, then straightens up.

GENERAL CROOK: I am not General Howard, dammit! I am none of these men! I am myself and I tried to help the Indian. I did what I could. You know damn well how I tried!

BIG FOOT stumbles forward into the spot, hugging himself, flapping his arms, blowing his fingers.

BIG FOOT: Oh it was cold, Colonel Forsyth, oh it was cold! You drove us hard remember, sir, God Almighty! Taking us to prison in Omaha. The night before the big killing you drank whisky because you had captured old Big Foot, already I was spitting blood and dead. But you drank on. In the morning you panicked and shot us, Colonel Forsyth.

GENERAL CROOK: I'm not Colonel Forsyth, dammit! I'm Crook!

BIG FOOT throws himself at the foot of the horse and lies in a grotesque posture, arms and legs raised.

BIG FOOT: This is how they found me, Colonel Forsyth. You shot us down and we froze like this, and this, and this… (*He mimes a series of poses.*) Why? We were poor, nearly dead with the great cold, I was leading what was left of my people to find peace. Why shoot old Big Foot? Was it our faces? Our smell? The way we sat our ponies when we had them? Were we vermin to be killed like rats in the barn? Where did you find this hatred?

GENERAL CROOK: Get up!

BIG FOOT: I am dead, Three-Stars. I am frozen! My limbs will not move.

GENERAL CROOK: This isn't fair! I tried to help! I did everything I could within the bounds of my duty as a soldier. Give me credit when it's due. Was there another soldier in the United States Army who tried to help the Indian like I did?

BIG FOOT crawls away, looking back at CROOK. Pause. STANDING BEAR steps forward and puts a hand on CROOK's arm.

STANDING BEAR: It is true.

GENERAL CROOK: Thank you, Standing Bear. Tell them what I did for the Poncas.

STANDING BEAR: In the Moon of the Red Grass Appearing the Great Father gave us a new reservation on the bank of the Arkansas. We walked a hundred and fifty miles to this place. Then we were all sick and many died. Soon I had one son left to die and he did die. When he was dying he made me promise to bury him in our old burial ground by the Swift Running Water. I put his body in a box and in a waggon and I took my dead son north. By that time it was the Snow Thaws Moon. The soldiers caught us and put us in the fort in chains.

GENERAL CROOK: I went to Fort Omaha to see them. I was appalled by the conditions under which the Poncas were being held.

STANDING BEAR: 'Gray Wolf,' I said to him then, 'I thought God intended us to live, but I was mistaken. God intends to give the country to the white people and we are to die. It may be well: it may be well.'

GENERAL CROOK: I went to the Press. I mounted a campaign. I went so far as to arrange a trial – Crook versus Standing Bear – whereby a judge would issue a writ of Habeas Corpus upon me to bring my Ponca prisoners into court and show by what authority I held them.

The vaulting horse is shoved off to alcove right. A judge's chair is brought on centre upper level. The CHIEFS crowd around the chair on the lower level, giving room for CROOK and STANDING BEAR. Enter JUDGE DUNDY, who takes the chair.

JUDGE DUNDY: This court is now in session. General George Crook, I have issued a writ of Habeas Corpus on you?

GENERAL CROOK: You have, your honour.

JUDGE DUNDY: Why are you holding Standing Bear of the Poncas as a prisoner?

GENERAL CROOK: He is off his reservation. He is an Indian.

JUDGE DUNDY: Who says he must stay on this 'reservation'?

GENERAL CROOK: The government. The government tells him where to live.

JUDGE DUNDY: But this man has no voice in the government?

GENERAL CROOK: He has no rights, your honour. The Fourteenth Amendment gave Negroes equal rights but not Indians. He is also, by law, an alien.

JUDGE DUNDY: How the hell can he be an alien if he was born here?

GENERAL CROOK: He is an Indian.

JUDGE DUNDY: Let's get this straight. You're saying that this man was born here, lives here, yet he's got no rights? That's not what the Declaration of Independence says, is it, General? Remember?

GENERAL CROOK: I do.

JUDGE DUNDY: Well, if you remember, let's have it.

GENERAL CROOK: (*Pause.*) We hold these truths to be self-evident: that all men are created equal...

JUDGE DUNDY: That's enough. So the case rests on one fine point. Is this person a man? Are you a man?

STANDING BEAR: I am a man.

JUDGE DUNDY: Then you have the right to avail yourself of the rights of freedom guaranteed by the Constitution.

GENERAL CROOK: But he is subject to government legislation concerning tribal Indians. They are a special case.

JUDGE DUNDY: (*Standing up.*) If you don't keep quiet, General, I'll make you a special case. You'll be the first General that I've fined a hundred dollars for contempt of court! Release Standing Bear! He is a free man!

The CHIEFS jump up and chair STANDING BEAR around the theatre in a wild demonstration. JUDGE DUNDY exits. GENERAL CROOK returns to his alcove. The CHIEFS bring STANDING BEAR back and resume their positions around the stage and auditorium. Pause.

CRAZY HORSE: One month later Great Warrior Sherman undid that law. He put aside this Constitution, he put aside these rights, he said that no Ponca was a man. It was Standing Bear's brother Big Snake who tried out this law again and the Army broke it. At Fort Reno they shot Big Snake dead and showed us the truth again. The Indian was an alien in his own land.

GENERAL CROOK: (*Sitting on his stool.*) I tried…

CRAZY HORSE: One half of you tried, the man. Then you were part Indian, but it did not last long.

The pianist plays the chords with full foatissimo and SITTING BULL steps into the spot. The drummers drum. SITTING BULL holds up his hand.

SITTING BULL: I am Tatanta Yotanka, the Sitting Bull, chief of the Hunkpapa Sioux and the most famous Indian of all time. There is no one here who has not heard of me! My deeds are known throughout the world. I have one story and it is not about my victories, my intellect, my powerful medicine, my numerous talents, my illustrions friends such as Buffalo Bill Cody and the Pope – my story is none of these. My story is a travel story. I was such a well-known figure in American politics that the Great White Father invited me to go to the East and I went to the great city of New York in the year of the white man's reckoning 1885. There I was taken for a journey on the waters and I saw a thing that amazed my eye and puzzled my mind – not an easy thing to do to Sitting Bull. On an island the whites had built a figure of a great squaw with a torch held up like this, and a book in her other hand. It was the biggest squaw I had ever seen, she touched the clouds. At her feet were broken chains. We sailed to the very ground on which the squaw stood and I was shown some writing on a mighty block of stone. It was a poem and it was long and I remember little poetry but my own, but I remember these words…

The CHIEFS sink to the ground, squat, hug themselves as if against the cold.

Give me your tired, your poor,
Your huddled masses yearning to breathe free.

Pause. SITTING BULL turns round and looks at CROOK.

SITTING BULL: You have seen this?

GENERAL CROOK: I have seen it.

SITTING BULL: Who is the squaw speaking to? Her face is towards the East, she looks across the sea.

GENERAL CROOK: (*Unable to look SITTING BULL in the eye.*) She talks to the whites who are unhappy in their own country. It is called the Statue of Liberty.

SITTING BULL: Ah, Liberty. Now I see. The squaw was therefore not including us. The puzzlement has gone.

He goes to walk awaddenly but suddenly turns on CROOK, his voice harsh and angry.

Do not tell me that you tried! We tried! We signed papers until our hands ached! We went to councils! We listened to commissioners! We gave you our land so we could have peace! You behaved as though you had given your word to children! The Great White Father killed his sons and daughters even when they were poor and in rags!

GENERAL CROOK: I respected you as men and warriors. What other recognition can a soldier give?

SITTING BULL: Crazy Horse, tell Three Stars God Almighty what his brother officer Sheridan said about The People.

CRAZY HORSE: He said that the only good Indian is a dead Indian.

SITTING BULL: By this time we were nearly all good Indians. We were all ready for death, until we heard the Word, the Ghost Dance.

WOVOKA takes the centre-stage, dancing. He acts like a mad prophet, full of passion and rage but clear and articulate.

He runs from centre round to all the CHIEFS, doing the strange side-to-side Ghost Dance. CROOK covers his eyes.

WOVOKA: Christ is an Indian! Who says Christ is white? I have sent for you to see me, the Messiah! I am going to talk to you about all your fathers and mothers, all your brothers and sisters who are dead. They are coming back. My children, I will teach you how to dance this dance and I want you to dance it. Get ready for your dance…

All the CHIEFS copy WOVOKA and follow him in the Ghost Dance. They do a big circle and resume their positions – now they are with WOVOKA, eager to hear what he has to say.

SITTING BULL: Hear him! Hear the Christ!

WOVOKA: In the beginning God made the earth and he sent Christ to teach the people but white men treated him badly, leaving scars on his body, and so he returned to Heaven. Now he has come back as an Indian. I will renew the earth and make it better! Dance!

The CHIEFS dance again, following WOVOKA, down the aisles, round the back of the auditorium, and return to the lower level. WOVOKA jumps onto the upper level.

The earth will have fresh soil! The fresh soil will bury the white men and then be covered with new grass, running water and trees. The buffalo will return. All you Indians who dance the Ghost Dance with me will rise into the air while this new world is in the making. When you are set down again all your dead friends will be with you. The land will belong to the Great Spirit again and he will give it to The People.

GENERAL CROOK: This is madness. This man's a charlatan, a hoaxer! Dammit, you can't put the clock back! Don't listen to him!

The CHIEFS form a circle round CROOK and do the Ghost Dance. The rhythm becomes insistent, deeper. The eyes of the CHIEFS glaze, they are dancing in a trance. Only CRAZY HORSE remains outside the circle.

WOVOKA: Who are The People?

CHIEFS: We are The People!

WOVOKA: Who is the Christ?

CHIEFS: You are the Christ!

GENERAL CROOK: In God's name, Crazy Horse, stop this mumbo-jumbo! Do you want another war on your hands?

CRAZY HORSE: Gray Wolf, if I had been allowed to live that long, if I had not been cut down with the bayonet while a prisoner…

GENERAL CROOK: That was not my doing!

CRAZY HORSE: You are all the pony-soldiers, Gray Wolf. You are all your people and we are ours. If I had lived in the time of the Ghost Dance, I would have done it! I would have danced! Even if I knew there was no chance of its being the Truth I would have been a Ghost Dancer and followed the prophet Wovoka!

GENERAL CROOK: This situation is getting out of control.

CRAZY HORSE: (*Leaping into the circle of Ghost Dancers.*) Hopo hook-ahay!

The rhythm mounts and the circle gets closer to CROOK. CRAZY HORSE leaps and twirls with a dance of his own but keeping in line. Suddenly he crouches and points a finger at CROOK. The dancers stop. Freeze.

CRAZY HORSE: You had come to our sacred ground, the centre of The People's world. The Black Hills were the last home of the Great Spirit and you came even there looking for gold! If I dug up the floors of your churches looking for metal, what would you do?

GENERAL CROOK: You couldn't expect us to take your religion seriously. It was mere superstition. There was no logic to it! Dammit!

CRAZY HORSE: Ha! Three in one and one in three. Virgin Mary with child!

CRAZY HORSE leaps into the air and the Ghost Dance starts again, creeping closer to the vaulting horse. The CHIEFS are now very close to CROOK, brushing his boots as they dance round him. CRAZY HORSE springs into the air and lands in a crouch, pointing at CROOK again. The dance pauses.

Who came after me up the Powder River into the holy Black Hills? Who helped the Great White Father break his word?

CHIEFS: Gray Wolf!

CRAZY HORSE: Who beat General Three Stars God Almighty Crook at the Battle of the Rosebud?

CHIEFS: Crazy Horse!

CRAZY HORSE: We loved the Black Hills, oh we loved that land. It was our heart and our middle. You came and fought us on behalf of thieves. You were paid by thieves! Where are the two men now? A soldier is a soldier and if his honour is sold for gold then that is the kind of soldier he is! If I had the naming of you I would have called you Golden Calf!

GENERAL CROOK strikes out at CRAZY HORSE in a rage. The CHIEFS crowd round him and pull him off the vaulting horse.

CRAZY HORSE jumps on his back and the CHIEFS force CROOK on to his hands and knees until CRAZY HORSE can get astride him as though on horseback. The CHIEFS then release CROOK and stand back. CRAZY HORSE laughs and digs his heels into CROOK's sides. CROOK behaves like a wild horse – he bucks, leaps, shakes, writhes, trying to dislodge his rider. The neighing the wild horse fills the theatre. CRAZY HORSE rides out the madness of CROOK until he is still.

CRAZY HORSE: Now I have you. You are the wild horse of my dream. You are the madness The People have tried to ride. I am on your back and you are quiet. At last I am riding my dream! But too late!

GENERAL CROOK: Let me get up, Crazy Horse!

CRAZY HORSE: No, you are the crazy horse. I am The People and I am going to ride your dreams for ever. You Americans, you Spaniards, you Englishmen, you Frenchmen and Dutchmen, you Portuguese, all of you are saddled with me. I am going to sit across your conscience and be your rider until the world ends.

GENERAL CROOK: This is a child's game! Dammit! Get off my back!

The CHIEFS spread out on either side of CROOK and CRAZY HORSE. They start making encouraging sounds, as if to a horse, clucking and whistling. CRAZY HORSE whacks CROOK over the backside.

CRAZY HORSE: Hopo-hook-ahay America! Giddiap! We should have ridden you before!

Slowly CROOK starts to shuffle forward with CRAZY HORSE on his back. The CHIEFS fall into line behind them. CROOK goes down the aisle on all fours. He moves very slowly and painfully. CRAZY HORSE starts the mourning song.

CRAZY HORSE: Where are the Tainos now?

CHIEFS: Where are the People?

CRAZY HORSE: Where are the Arawaks?

CHIEFS: Where are the People?

CRAZY HORSE: Where are the Aztecs?

CHIEFS: Where are the People?

CRAZY HORSE: Where are the Incas?

> *As the CHIEFS go down the aisle they should try to involve the audience in the mourning song 'Where are the People?' At the same time the pianist mounts the upper level, finds the white-wash and brush and paints in the remaining portions of the Americas.*

CHIEFS: Where are the People?

> *The refrain is repeated after each tribe.*

CRAZY HORSE: Where are the Tainos?
Where are the Arawaks?
Where are the Aztecs?
Where are the Incas?
Where are the Wampanoags?
Where are the Pequots?
Where are the Narragansets?
Where are the Ottawas?
Where are the Shawnees?
Where are the Miamis?
Where are the Foxes?
Where are the Chitimichas?
Where are the Taenzas?
Where are the Natchez?
Where are the Karoks?
Where are the Yazoos?
Where are the Choctaws?

Where are the Chickasaws?
Where are the Bilox?
Where are the Seminoles?
Where are the Apalachees?
Where are the Modocs?
Where are the Apaches?
Where are the Mohaves?
Where are the Paiutes?
Where are the Shastas?
Where are the Yuma?
Where are the Navahoes?
Where are the Utes?
Where are the Osages?
Where are the Pawnees?
Where are the Poncas?
Where are the Santees?
Where are the Cheyennes?
Where are the Teton Sioux?
Where are the Arapahoes?
Where are the Kiowas?
Where are the Comanches?
Where are the Nez Percés?
Where are the Brulés?
Where are the Minneconjous?
Where are the Oglala Sioux?
Where are the People?

As the last CHIEF exits, the pianist paints in the last portion of the map. He then exits. By this time the lights have dimmed down and only the moon is illuminated. It darkens, goes out.

The End.